Live
life
simply

Edited by
Jeffrey Young

Author Allegra Strategies
Design John Osborne and Gina Serfontein
Publisher Allegra Publications Ltd.

Visit our website:
allegra-publishing.com

Published by Allegra Publications Ltd © 2020

Serendipity House, 106 Arlington Road, London, NW1 7HP, UK.

10 human principles for a simply better life

1   **The principle of focus**
2   The principle of strength
3   The principle of choice
4   The principle of health
5   The principle of understanding
6   **The principle of humility**
7   The principle of bravery
8   The principle of appreciation
9   **The principle of laughter**
10 **The principle of friendship**

Change will not come
if we wait for some other
person or some other time.
We are the ones we have
been waiting for.
We are the change
we seek.

BARACK OBAMA

1

The principle of

focus

is knowing what you want most of all and setting clear goals to achieve your chosen destiny. Focus takes careful planning to prioritise emphasis on the most important outcomes with limited distraction. Success requires a positive mindset, taking good risk and getting things done efficiently but with less haste.

What will you do today
that will matter tomorrow?

Some people dream of success,
while others wake up and work hard at it.

2

The principle of
strength

relates to maintaining inner control in challenging circumstances and deep periods of adversity. Strength requires preparation, hard work and self-sacrifice and finding personal mechanisms to hold strong and keep focused on true needs. It's about never giving up on what is most important (unless it is wise to do so) and taking full responsibility for your actions, the consequences of these actions, and the impact you will have on others.

Good habits are worth
being fanatical about.

JOHN IRVING

If I had eight hours to chop down a tree,
I'd spend the first four hours
sharpening the axe.

ABRAHAM LINCOLN

If you don't have time to do it right,
when will you have time to do it over?

JOHN WOODEN

Hardships often prepare ordinary people for an extraordinary destiny.

C.S. LEWIS

Discipline is choosing between
what you want now
and what you want the most.

ABRAHAM LINCOLN

Difficult roads often lead
to beautiful destinations.

Ask not for a lighter load
but broader shoulders.

JEWISH PROVERB

Do not judge me by my successes,
judge me by how many times I fell down
and got back up again.

NELSON MANDELA

Don't raise your voice,
improve your argument.

The comeback is stronger
than the setback.

DR. JILL MURRAY

Sometimes a stumble prevents a fall.

ENGLISH PROVERB

Don't let anyone tell you
you cannot do it;
especially not yourself.

3

The principle of
choice

The economic principle of life is that time is short and our resources are limited. We must therefore make choices with full knowledge that we can't do everything and that the choices we make lead us away to other pathways and people, and to some we may never return. Sometimes strength is in letting go rather than hanging on fearfully to what we know. There is freedom and power in knowing that we can declutter and delayer from material things and remove toxicity from our world with our resolute choices towards a purer, healthier, more meaningful lifestyle.

Time is precious.
Waste it wisely.

Identify the essential.
Eliminate the rest.

LEO BABAUTA

There are only three questions
you need to ask yourself in life.
Who am I? Where am I going?
Who is coming with me?
And you must ask them
in that very order.

Folks are usually about as happy
as they make their minds up to be.

ABRAHAM LINCOLN

While there is no single recipe for success, trying to please everyone is a certain recipe for failure.

Don't sweat the small stuff.

MOTHER TO A SON

Some things you cannot change,
but you can change your attitude to them.

#31

Holding on to anger
is like drinking poison
and expecting the other person to die.

BUDDHA

Avoid negative people;
they have a problem
for every solution.

ALBERT EINSTEIN

Sometimes it's letting go
that shows strength,
not always holding on.

HERMAN HESSE

You can never start a new chapter in your life if you keep re-reading the last one.

I am confident that nobody
will accuse me of selfishness
if I ask to spend time
while I am still in good health,
with my family, my friends,
and also with myself.

NELSON MANDELA

The principle of
choice

4

The principle of
health

is much more than embracing healthy eating and physical exercise. Health is a philosophy of living in balanced symphony with yourself and within nature. Sleep, relaxation, positive reflection and being surrounded by people who uplift you are key to maintaining that healthy spirit of self-worth and harmony. A healthy body and healthy mind provide a strong base to achieve positive impact for yourself and for all the world around you.

A good life is waking up an hour early to live an hour more.

I have decided to be happy
because it's good for my health.

VOLTAIRE

Investing in health is the best investment you will ever make.

If you think Wellness is expensive,
try illness.

Never did Nature say one thing
and Wisdom say another.

EDMUND BURKE

Your body hears everything
your mind says.

NAOMI JUDD

An apple a day keeps the doctor away.

Doctors won't make you healthy.
Nutritionists won't make you slim.
Teachers won't make you smart.
Gurus won't make you calm.
Mentors won't make you rich.
Trainers won't make you fit.
Ultimately, you have to take responsibility.

NAVAL RAVIKANT

The principle of
health

Every next level of your life
will demand a different you.

You come into this world with nothing
and will leave with nothing,
so don't get too obsessed over possessions.

THOMAS McCAFFERY

An honest man's pillow
is his peace of mind.

Always sleep on big decisions.

5

The principle of

understanding

is built on compassion, empathy and unconditional kindness. The open-minded, generous listener seeks first to understand then to be understood and shows respect to people of all ages, all levels and all walks of life. The wisdom gained through understanding the journey of others is a sure pathway to a more peaceful life.

Seek first to understand,
then to be understood.

STEPHEN COVEY

The principle of
understanding

I have learned that people
will forget what you said,
people will forget what you did,
but people will never forget
how you made them feel.

MAYA ANGELOU

What counts more than talent,
energy or concentration,
or commitment or anything else
is kindness...
All the big words – virtue, justice, truth –
are dwarfed by the greatness of kindness.

STEPHEN FRY

The principle of
understanding

Everyone you meet is fighting a battle
you know nothing about.
Be kind. Always.

ROBIN WILLIAMS

Listening is one of the highest forms of respect.

It is only with the heart
that one sees rightly.
What is essential
is invisible to the eye.

THE LITTLE PRINCE, ANTOINE DE SAINT-EXUPÉRY

The principle of
understanding

The real voyage of discovery consists not in seeking new landscapes, but in having new eyes.

MARCEL PROUST

Most smiles are started by another smile.

Our days are happier when we give people a piece of our heart rather than a piece of our mind.

No one heals themselves
by wounding another.

If you can do no good,
at least do no harm.

KURT VONNEGUT

Those who really matter
don't care about how much
you have, know or earn,
they only care about
how much you care.

#60

6

The principle of
humility

is understanding that our place in this world is minuscule in relation to the grandness of the Universe. But rather than our existence being futile or irrelevant, we have the magic power to profoundly impact others by our actions or inactions in each moment of life. The moral compass of humility rests on the fundamental concept of respect and acting on the belief that all beings are created and valued equally.

True humility
is not thinking less of yourself;
it is thinking of yourself less.

How you make others feel about themselves
says a lot about you.

The only person you should try to be better than is the person that you were yesterday.

Do not spoil what you have by desiring what you have not.
Remember what you have now is once what you dreamed of.

EPICURUS

Be humble with the wealth and status you have acquired. Imagine you halve it, then halve it again; that's a true reflection of your humanity.

LUIS ORTIZ BASUALDO

Success is a lousy teacher.
It seduces smart people
into thinking they can't lose.

BILL GATES

Respect is how you treat everyone,
not just those you want to impress.

RICHARD BRANSON

**The principle of
humility**

Never look down on anyone
unless you are helping them up.

JESSE JACKSON

The ultimate human success
is inspiring others to achieve greatness.

Talent wins games,
but teamwork wins championships.

MICHAEL JORDAN

There is no limit to what a person can do if they don't mind who gets the credit for it.

PLAQUE IN PRESIDENT RONALD REAGAN'S OFFICE

The only respect you ever get
is the respect you earn.

7

The principle of

bravery

is having the confidence, self-belief and authenticity to be the best you in all circumstances. It takes sheer courage to take action when change is needed and to make a strong personal stand that reflects your core life values. One of the biggest risks in life is never to take a risk. We often regret more the decisions we didn't take than the mistakes we made. Now is the time to begin the project that you always wanted, to visit that place you always dreamed of and to start that conversation you always yearned for.

Listen to your teachers
and never be afraid to put your hand up.

HOMELESS PERSON IN LONDON

Every accomplishment starts
with the decision to try.

JOHN F. KENNEDY

When was the last time
you did something for the first time?
What if you fly?

Be yourself,
everybody else is already taken.

OSCAR WILDE

You're only given a little spark of madness.
You mustn't lose it.

ROBIN WILLIAMS

The principle of
bravery

Stand up for what you believe in,
even if it means standing alone.

ANDY BIERSACK

I learned that courage was not the absence of fear, but the triumph over it.
The brave man is not he who does not feel afraid, but he who conquers that fear.

NELSON MANDELA

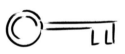

Unless you realise that you have the power to say 'No' you never have the power to truly say 'Yes'.

DAN MILLMAN

It takes a lot of courage to forgive someone, but it takes even more courage to ask forgiveness.

If you are lucky enough
to find a way of life you love,
you have to find the courage to live it.

JOHN IRVING

Something counter-intuitive that I have learned is that showing vulnerability as a leader can often be seen as a strength.

JACINDA ARDERN

Who says your dreams
should just stay your dreams?

8

The principle of

appreciation

is about living each moment with positive
awareness, enjoyment and gratitude. Living the
now is essential because life is so fragile and time
flashes past before our eyes – and often before
our hearts have time to express our deepest inner
feelings. The time to live and love is now, the
present is a present – enjoy and be grateful for
every precious moment.

Enjoy the little things,
for one day you may look back
and realise they were the big things.

ROBERT BRAULT

Today is a great day to have a great day.

The time to love is now.

LEO BUSCAGLIA

If not now, when?

Life is not measured by the number of breaths that you take, but by the moments that take your breath away.

MAYA ANGELOU

It's the simple things in life
that are the most extraordinary.

PAULO COELHO

The time you enjoy wasting
is not wasted time.

I count the sunny hours.

EKKE BEINSSEN

Don't forget to stop and smell the roses.

MOTHER TO A SON

Time is precious –
cherish your children.

WOMAN ON A PLANE

We don't stop playing because we grow old.
We grow old because we stop playing.

GEORGE BERNARD SHAW

Don't cry because it's over,
smile because it happened.

DR. SEUSS

9

The principle of

laughter

is sharing and expressing pure enjoyment in concert with those around us. Humour and fun promote positivity in good times and build memories and resilience for periods of adversity. Having the capacity to laugh at oneself shows true strength of character, and the ability to make others laugh is one of the greatest gifts of humanity. We are all in this life together and life is most enjoyable when we are laughing or smiling with others.

Birthdays are good for your health.
Studies show that people who have
more birthdays live longer.

If you think I'm screwed up, you should meet the rest of my family.

Never laugh at your wife's choices.
Remember you are one of them.

When people are laughing
they're generally not killing one another.

ALAN ALDA

A loyal friend laughs at your jokes
when they're not so good,
and sympathizes with your problems
when they're not so bad.

ARNOLD H. GLASOW

Perfect men are like unicorns.
Everybody talks about them.
Nobody has ever seen one.

My ex and I divorced for religious reasons.
He thought he was God and I didn't.

The older I get, the better I used to be.

JOHN McENROE

I'd be happy to live to 80
as long as I was comfortable
and in good health.
Mind you, ask me again
on the eve of my 80th birthday.

BONNIE TYLER

I tried to behave, but there were too many other options.

Those who were seen dancing were
thought to be mad by those
who could not hear the music.

FRIEDRICH NIETZSCHE

Remember to smile. It really suits you.

CLAYTON, NEWSPAPER MAN, NYC

10

The principle of
friendship

is fundamental to 'the human experience'. The Holstee Manifesto says: 'Life is about the people you meet and the things you create with them'. Nature reminds us to surround ourselves with people who uplift, complement and share our values. To be a friend, we must reciprocate with empathy, listening and true time commitment. Teamwork and collaboration help to achieve more than any individual can alone, and give the opportunity to live a richer, more fulfilling existence. Where possible, success – and even darker moments – are far better shared than experienced alone.

If you want to go fast, go alone.
If you want to go far, go together.

AFRICAN PROVERB

Friendship and collaboration
can change a nation.

MJELI LONBA

True friendship isn't a big thing.
It's a million little things.

Friends are those rare people
who ask how we are
and then wait to hear the answer.

ED CUNNINGHAM

#112

If you go looking for a friend,
you're going to find they're very scarce.
If you go out to be a friend,
you'll find them everywhere.

ZIG ZIGLAR

If you love someone, set them free.
If they come back, they are yours;
if they don't, they never were.

RICHARD BACH

The people who want to stay in your life will always find a way.

Those who don't judge you
are the only ones who really matter.
Those who do, don't matter.

It is not a lack of love,
but a lack of friendship
that makes unhappy marriages.

FRIEDRICH NIETZSCHE

**The principle of
friendship**

Laughter is the shortest distance between two people.

VICTOR BORGE

Friends are a good way
of apologising for family.

When you're in jail,
a good friend will be trying to bail you out.
Your best friend will be there in the cell
with you saying 'that was fun'.

GROUCHO MARX

The principle of friendship

#120

Use your smile to change the world. Don't let the world change your smile.

More from Allegra Publishing

The Meaning of Coffee

The Meaning of Chocolate

The Meaning of Wine

The Meaning of Meow

The Meaning of Husbands

The London Coffee Guide

The New York Coffee Guide

The Los Angeles Coffee Guide

The Coffee Guide app

The London Wellness Guide

Allegra
PUBLISHING